JOURNEY INTO CIVILIZATION
THE VIKINGS

by Robert Nicholson and Claire Watts

CHELSEA JUNIORS

A division of ███████████████ Publishers
████████████████

Editorial Consultant: Gareth Binns, Education Officer,
York Archaeological Trust and Coucil for British Archaeology

ISBN 0-7910-2709-0
ISBN 0-7910-2733-3 (pbk.)

Printed in Hong Kong by Wing King Tong Co. Ltd.

Photographic credits:
Werner Forman: p3, p6, p7, p8, p9, p10, p11, p12, p13, p16, p17,p.20(top), p.21, p23, p30(top), p32(bottom);
Toby Maudsley: p20(craft), p22; Ronald Sheridan: p.30(middle); York Archaeological Trust: p.19,p.24

Illustration credits:
Kevind Maddison: p9,p11,pp12-13,p14,p17,pp18-19,pp22-23,p24
Maxine Hamil cover: p25-29

Contents

All words that appear in **bold** can be found in the glossary.

Eric the Red founded a settlement in Greenland.

▲ The Vikings were the first Europeans to reach America.

Lindisfarne was an island whose wealthy, unprotected monastery was an easy target for the Vikings.

"on 8 june the ravages of heathen men miserably destroyed god's church on lindisfarne with plunder and slaughter ..."

(ANGLO-SAXON CHRONICLE, 793)

The Viking World

The first glimpse many European people had of the Vikings was when the Viking longships appeared off their coasts. No one was prepared for the invading warriors and few countries could resist the Vikings. From the first attacks in 793, Viking raids were a frequent occurrence all over northwestern Europe for the next 200 years.

◀ Vikings settled in Iceland in the ninth century.

▼ The Vikings who settled in this area were called Rus. The name Russia comes from this word.

▲ The French king gave the province of Normandy to a Viking duke named Rollo to try to stop him from attacking the French coast.

▲ Constantinople was the main city of the powerful **Byzantine empire**. The Vikings traded there.

Viking Lands

The Vikings came from the countries that are now called Sweden, Norway and Denmark. These lands are cold and bleak, with deep rivers, rocky coasts and towering mountains. Even though the Vikings fished and hunted wild animals, there was not enough good farm land to produce food for all of them.

Many Vikings chose to set out to seek a better life using their skills as seamen and warriors.

Viking lands were divided into several different kingdoms. The richest and most powerful men became leaders, and were called kings and dukes. These leaders would sometimes call all the **free men** to a meeting known as the **Allthing**, where they would discuss plans about expeditions to other countries or make decisions about local problems. There were often wars between the different kingdoms, particularly over pieces of good land.

▼ Men gathering for the Allthing.

▼ The narrow, deep-watered **fjords** of **Scandinavia** form perfect natural harbors.

Pirates or Traders?

Pirates

The Vikings attacked the lands around them, particularly Britain and France. They stole food and treasures and carried people off to become slaves. People who lived in isolated areas on the coast or on islands were terrified of the Vikings' attacks. They were mostly farmers, and were not used to defending themselves and their families. They added to their daily prayers the words "God deliver us from the fury of the **Northmen**."

▲ Viking helmets like this one have been found at a number of gravesites in Europe. Soldiers were often buried with all their weapons because the Vikings believed they would need them on the way to heaven.

▼ Rope was wrapped around the hilt of Viking swords to protect the warrior's hand.

Traders

In certain places, the Vikings got food and goods by trading rather than by attacking and stealing property. They usually chose to trade rather than attack when the inhabitants were stronger or more organized and could defend themselves better. Viking traders traveled as far south as the Black Sea trading their furs, jewelry and slaves for spices and wine.

▶ Goods were sold for a weight of gold or silver coins rather than for a number of coins. Merchants used tiny portable scales to weigh the gold or silver. If they needed to give change they would break up the coins.

Longships

The Vikings were superb seamen and used ships for traveling on the lakes, seas and fjords of Scandinavia — as well as for trips farther away from home. The ships were measured by the number of oars they had. The smallest, a faering, had four and the largest, a longship, had about 32. A big longship might be nearly 100 feet long and would travel at up to 20 miles per hour under full sail. Ships were so important to the Vikings that their language contained dozens of ways of saying "ship."

The Vikings managed to navigate without any of the modern equipment that is used today. They found their way by watching the stars and sun, as well as familiar landmarks like islands and mountains. They also looked for birds that are found in different places at different times of year, like puffins and fulmars.

▲ Viking ships were among the first to have a **keel**, which helped them to cut through the water very fast and made them stable even in rough weather.

▲ Oars were used if the sail was not up, when there was no wind or on inland waters. Each rower sat on a box that held his belongings and a waterproof reindeer-skin sleeping bag.

▶ The gaps between the oak planks of the ship were made waterproof by filling them with sheep's wool dipped in tar.

◀ The ship used one huge square sail. In bad weather this was lowered over the ship and then fastened down like a tent to protect the men inside. The sail was made of thick, coarse material.

◀ The **prow** of a Viking ship was elaborately carved, usually with the head of a dragon or another animal. The ships had names that reflected the shape of their prows, like "Long Serpent," "Snake of the Sea," and "Horse of the Home of Ice."

Heroes

The Vikings admired bold and fearless men and their heroes were all soldiers, sailors or explorers. The deeds of heroes were told again and again until they became more like **myths** than historical fact.

Leif Ericson

Eric the Red's son Leif, who was known as "Lucky," arrived in northern America 500 years before Columbus reached the continent. He landed south of Newfoundland in a place he named Markland. He then traveled to Vinland, which may have been south of what is now New York. After two years in America, the Vikings were attacked by Native Americans defending their land. The Vikings left soon after.

King Cnut

By 1016 England had suffered 200 years of Viking raids, which had made the country very weak. In that year, the English king died, making it easy for King Cnut of Denmark to take over. The English accepted him because he was a wise ruler and brought peace.

Harald Haardraade

As the fame of the Vikings spread throughout Europe, many kings paid Vikings to work in their armies. The Byzantine emperor had an elite fighting force of Vikings called the **Varangarian Guard**. Harald Haardraade, or Hard-nose, was a famous member of the Guard, later became king of Norway. He was the last Viking to land with an army in England.

Sagas and Runes

Viking children did not go to school to learn. Instead, lessons came in the form of long stories, or **sagas**, told by traveling storytellers at feasts and festivals. Sagas told the adventures of the gods or of great Viking heroes. These stories were important ways of teaching history, geography and navigation. Sagas were especially appreciated on dark, cold winter nights, when everyone sat inside around the fire.

Children would also learn while helping their parents around the house and farm.

▲ Some buildings were decorated with pictures from famous sagas. The wood carving above shows Sigurd the Dragon-Slayer attacking a dragon.

▲ This stone carving shows one of the tales of Odin, the Vikings' god of war. You can see Odin in the center at the top, handing a sword to an old man.

The Futhark

The Viking alphabet, the **futhark**, was very different from ours. The letters, or **runes**, were made up mostly of straight lines. This is because they were usually carved into wood or stone, and it is easier to carve straight lines than curves.

▶ These are all the runes of the futhark. Underneath you can see which letters of our alphabet correspond to each rune. Try writing your name in runes – it's like a secret code!

a b c d e f g h

ij k l m n o p q

r s t u v w x y z

15

The Viking Gods

The Vikings believed that there were lots of different gods who lived in a place called **Asgard**. Each god was responsible for a different thing, like war, travel or the home. These gods were not perfect. They had very human qualities, and also human weaknesses like jealousy and greed.

If a Viking died fighting it was believed that he went to a hall in Asgard called **Valhalla**, where everybody fought all day and feasted all night.

Some Important Gods

Odin

Freyja

Thor

THOR, the god of thunder, was the most popular god. He had a quick temper, and was a little stupid, but very good-hearted. He had the qualities that the Vikings valued most: strength and determination.

ODIN, or Woden, was the god of war, who rode an eight-legged horse. He often doubted himself and spent too long trying to decide whether to do things or not.

FREY made sure that the sun shined, the rain fell and the crops grew. He owned a magic boat that could carry all the gods at once, but that he kept folded up in his pocket the rest of the time.

FREYJA was Frey's sister. She was the goddess of love and war. She could turn herself into a bird by putting on a magic falcon skin.

LOKI was half god, half fire-spirit. He caused the other gods a lot of trouble.

▲ When Viking warriors died their bodies were often placed in longships, which were buried, or set on fire and pushed out to sea.

▶ Towards the end of the Viking age, the Vikings began to convert to Christianity. This is a mold made in the tenth century for making Christian crosses, but it was also used for making copies of **Mjollnir**, Thor's hammer.

At Home

The Vikings were not only skilled soldiers, seamen and traders. Most Vikings were farmers who lived with their families, growing and making all the things they needed for their daily lives. Children helped their parents as soon as they were able to. Even very small children had their own jobs around the farm, like feeding the animals or gathering firewood.

Viking women worked on the farm and wove material for clothes and blankets on small looms. When their husbands were away fighting, they took care of the whole farm.

Viking houses were made of timber planks and woven branches, with turf or thatched roofs. Stone was used in places where there was no wood, like Shetland and Iceland. Inside, the houses were not divided into rooms. Areas were separated by stretching cloth or skins between the pillars which supported the roof.

A typical farm would contain the family house, or more than one house if the family were large. There were also sheds for the animals, a workshop with a furnace for making metal tools and small huts for slaves.

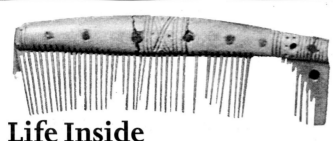

Life Inside

● Viking homes were very dark because they had no windows to let in light.

● It was difficult to keep them clean because cattle had to be kept indoors to protect them from the cold.

● Vikings often suffered from head lice, so most people had combs.

Games

Viking children did not spend all their time helping their parents. They had some time to themselves for playing games and carving wooden toys. Girls and boys went skating in winter, using skates carved from bone. These were strapped to the children's shoes with strips of leather.

When it was too dark and cold to go outside, Viking children may have played a game called **hnefatal**. This was a board game similar to chess, but with simple pieces, like checkers.

Crafts

Vikings were very skilled craftsmen, making marvelous objects from stone, wood and metal. Many of the most beautiful objects were not made by artists, but by ordinary people. A farmer might make a brooch using the same furnace he used to make his plough. Because there were no banks, people wore their wealth in the form of jewelry. This was the best way to keep it safe.

Smiths were very highly respected and often became very wealthy. Thor, one of the most important Viking gods, used a smith's hammer as his main weapon.

▲ Some jewelry was made especially to be buried with a dead person. This arm-ring was found at a burial site.

Make Some Viking Jewelry

Look at the decoration on the Viking objects in this book. Can you see how all the figures are woven around each other? The Vikings loved to use complicated patterns for decoration.

Try making a bracelet or brooch from modeling clay using Viking designs.

◄ Use four small balls of clay to make the heads.

▼ Roll out three long strands and braid them together.

20

▼ This is a mold that was used to make part of a helmet. Once the mold was made, many helmets could be made with this pattern.

▶ This gold pendant was worn around the neck as a magical charm. Look at the elaborate patterns that cover it.

▶ The symbol of Thor's hammer was used in much Viking jewelry. This silver hammer head is ornate, but many were much simpler than this.

Food

Finding food was a very important part of the Vikings' life. Little of the land was fertile and the winters were very long and harsh. They usually ate rich stews of beef or lamb from animals they raised on their farms, but they also fished and hunted. They grew vegetables like cabbage, peas and beans and also ate wild leeks and garlic.

Picnic tables would be set up in the middle of the room for meals, and members of the family would sit on the same wooden benches that they slept on at night. They ate off rectangular wooden platters or from soapstone bowls, using spoons and the knives that were carried on their belts at all times.

The Vikings used drinking horns as well as cups. Because the horns did not have flat bottoms, they had to be passed around the table until they were empty. A man who could empty a drinking horn in one turn was admired. The usual drink was mead, a sweet beer made from honey.

Food Facts

● When the Vikings had no other grain they would use peas to make bread.
● Salt was made by boiling sea water.
● The Vikings ate two meals a day: the day meal after the early farmwork and the night meal at the end of the day.

▼ Cooking was done over an open hearth fire. Meat was roasted on huge spits, and stews were made in big iron cauldrons. Sometimes a **gridiron** made of coiled iron was used. Does it remind you of part of a modern stove? Bread was baked in stone ovens or in the ashes of the fire.

▼ Bowls were made from pottery or soapstone.

Thor was furious at the Giant King's rudeness, but it did not seem a very good idea to lose his temper when he was surrounded by giants.

"What skill would you like to challenge us with?" continued the Giant King.

Thor looked around him at the giants.

"I doubt if anyone here can drink as much as I can," Thor replied.

The Giant King signaled to a servant, who brought forward a huge drinking horn.

"This is the horn used by all my followers," he said. "A good drinker can finish it in one try, and all here can down it in two at the most. Let us see what the great Thor can do!"

Thor took the horn. It was certainly not the largest he had ever drunk from. He raised it to his mouth and began to swallow the water. He felt sure he could drink it all, but he ran out of breath before the horn was empty. He looked into the horn and found that it was no less full than before. He drank a second time, and again had to stop for breath. This time the horn was no longer brimming full. He took a third drink, gulping down the liquid until he was sure he must have emptied the horn, but although the level was lower than before, the horn was by no means empty.

"You don't seem to be much of a drinker," said the Giant King. "Why not try your strength? Some of the younger giants like to test themselves by lifting my cat. We don't think this much of a feat, but perhaps you'd like to try?"

Standing beside the Giant King's chair was the most enormous cat Thor had ever seen. He braced himself and then put both arms under the cat and heaved. The cat simply arched its back. Thor heaved again and managed to make the cat lift one paw off the ground before he had to admit defeat.

"As I thought," said the Giant King scornfully. "You may be strong in Asgard and in the realms of men, but your strength is nothing here."

Thor grew angry at this. "I can match any of your men in a fight. Just let anyone here wrestle with me."

There was a roar of laughter from all the giants in the hall.

"Everyone here feels that wrestling with you would be too easy," said the Giant King. "Perhaps you could fight Elli, my foster mother."

A wrinkled old woman hobbled forward leaning on a stick. Thor thought that the Giant King was making fun of him until Elli threw down her stick and took hold of him. He knew at once that his strength would be sorely tested. They struggled and fought, but eventually Elli threw Thor off balance so that he landed on one knee.

"Enough, enough!" shouted the giant King. "You have shown us that you have no strength as a wrestler either. As you pose no threat to us, you may eat with us and spend the night here in Utgard."

Thor and his companions were very hungry and tired after their long journey. When they had eaten, the tables were pushed back, and they spread their bedding in a space on the floor among the giants.

Thor awoke early, before any of the giants, and roused his companions.

"Come, let's go before the giants wake up," he whispered.

They tiptoed over the sleeping giants and out of the gates of Utgard. To their surprise, they found the Giant King already outside waiting for them. He walked with them across the plain for a while.

At last he stopped: "This is where I must leave you. Thor, do not feel too upset about your failures last night."

Thor was puzzled. "But I have never before been so badly beaten," he said.

The Giant King replied: "You were not competing in a fair fight. I feared your strength, so I used magic to deceive you. The other end of the horn that you drank from was in the sea. When you reach the shore you will see just how much you have lowered its level. The cat you lifted was really the giant serpent whose body is wrapped around the world. You managed to lift it until its back touched the sky. And as for Elli, it was a wonder you withstood her for so long. You see, Elli is Old Age, which defeats all men in time."

Thor was furious that he had been tricked. He seized his hammer Mjollnir and swung it around his head, but the Giant King and Utgard had vanished, as if they had never been there.

29

How We Know

Have you ever wondered how, although the Vikings lived over 1000 years ago, we know so much about their daily lives?

Evidence from the Ground

Certain objects have been found preserved in wet earth or water. Often these are very ordinary objects which were thrown away by the Vikings because they were broken or not needed. Archaeologists have pieced them together and figured out how they were used.

Some important Vikings were buried in ships full of their possessions. When these ships are discovered, archaeologists gain valuable information about the Vikings.

Evidence from Books

Many of the stories told by the Vikings were written down, and so it is very easy to find out who the important gods were and what various historical figures did. We even know that when Eric the Red discovered Greenland, he gave it that name in spite of its cold iciness because "many would want to go there if it had so promising a name."

Evidence Around Us

Many place names in Europe originally had Viking names, and so we can tell where the Vikings settled.

The whole of Normandy in France was taken over by the Vikings, and the name means land of the Northmen.

In Great Britain many place names have the Viking endings "-thorpe" and "-by," like Scunthorpe and Grimsby.

And what about our days of the week? Did you know that Wednesday was originally Woden's day, and Thursday Thor's day?

Glossary

Allthing
A council of free men that met when problems arose. This was the only form of government the Vikings had.

Asgard
The place where the Vikings believed that their gods lived, and where they would go when they died.

Byzantine empire
The strongest world power at the time of the Vikings. The Byzantine empire lasted from the 6th to the 15th century, and was also known as the East Roman Empire.

free men
All the men who were not slaves. Slaves were usually people who had been captured on raids.

fjords
Narrow inlets between high cliffs.

futhark
The runic alphabet used by the Vikings. The word is taken from the sound of the first six letters.

gridiron
A coiled metal strip that was placed in the fire to heat pots on.

hnefatal
A board game played by the Vikings.

keel
The long timber that forms the lowest part of a ship and helps give it balance.

Mjollnir
Thor's hammer. He carried it with him at all times.

myths
Traditional stories about gods or heroes. Myths reveal what the people who tell them think about the world and how it works.

Northmen
Most of the people the Vikings attacked or traded with knew them as "Northmen." "Viking" was a term they used to describe themselves.

prow
The front end of a ship.

runes
The letters of the Viking alphabet. Runes are made up of straight lines because they were intended to be carved on wood or stone.

saga
Storytelling adventures of gods or heroes. Although sagas were usually passed on by word of mouth, some were written down.

Scandinavia
The group of countries that include Denmark, Norway, Sweden and Iceland.

Valhalla
The hall in Asgard where warriors hoped to go when they died. There they could fight all day and feast all night.

Varangarian Guard
A section of the Byzantine army made up of Vikings. The Varangarian Guard were the emperor's bodyguard.

Index